3637 2398

W9-BUY-047

I LIKE **REPTILES** AND **AMPHIBIANS!**

FUN FACTS ABOUT
FROGS!

Carmen Bredeson

Enslow Elementary

an imprint of

Enslow Publishers, Inc.

40 Industrial Road
Box 398
Berkeley Heights, NJ 07922
USA

http://www.enslow.com

CONTENTS

WORDS TO KNOW

life cycle (SY cuhl)—The different steps in an animal's life.

lungs (LUHNGZ)—Part of the body that breathes air.

habitat (HA bih tat)—The place where an animal or plant lives and grows.

tadpole (TAD pohl)—First stage in the life of a frog.

vocal cords (VOH cuhl KORDZ)—Part of the throat where sound is made.

PARTS OF A FROG

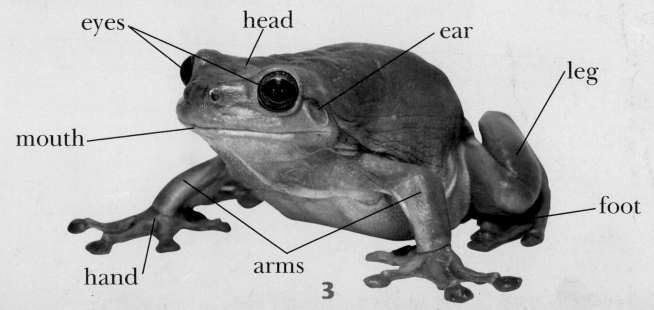

eyes

head

ear

leg

mouth

hand

arms

foot

3

WHERE DO FROGS LIVE?

Most frogs live in places that are warm and wet. Some frogs live in water. Others live on land. Most spend part of their time in water and part on land. There are even frogs that live high up in the trees.

WHAT DO FROGS EAT?

Frogs eat things such as spiders, bugs, earthworms, and snails. The frog's sticky tongue shoots out.

White's Tree Frog

It grabs a bug walking or flying by. The frog holds the wiggling bug in its mouth. Gulp! The frog swallows its meal whole.

A Green Frog eats a dragonfly.

WHAT EATS FROGS?

Many animals eat frogs. A few of them are birds, fish, snakes, and bats. Some frogs jump into the water to get away from danger. Others change colors and hide in the leaves. Many frogs are the same color as their **habitat** where they live. Where did that frog go?

Argentine Horned Frog

Can you find the frog in this picture?

IS IT A FROG OR A TOAD?

Most frogs have smooth skin. They have long back legs for leaping.

frog

Most toads have bumpy skin. They have shorter back legs for walking. Sometimes it is hard to tell a frog from a toad. In fact, toads are really a kind of frog.

toad

Painted Reed Frog

This frog has air in its throat.

DO FROGS
MAKE SOUNDS?

Some frogs sound like barking dogs or quacking ducks. A frog pushes air from its **lungs** to its throat. Sounds come out as the air goes over the **vocal cords**. Usually, big frogs make low sounds and little frogs make high sounds.

WHY DO
FROGS
LOSE THEIR SKIN?

Frog skin does not get bigger as the frog grows. When the skin gets too small, new skin grows under the old skin. The frog uses its front feet to pull off the old skin like a sweater. Some frogs eat their old skin.

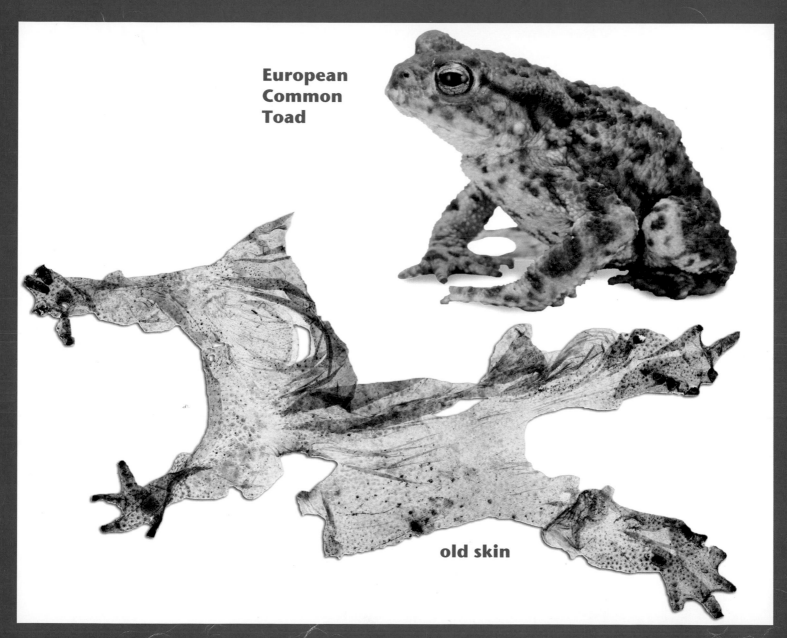

European Common Toad

old skin

HOW DO
FROGS
JUMP SO HIGH?

Frogs have long back legs that fold up. When a frog wants to jump, its legs unfold and shoot straight out. The frog goes up, high in the air. Some frogs can leap ten feet.

WHICH FROG IS THE BIGGEST?

The biggest frog is the Goliath Frog of West Africa. It can grow to be the size of a small dog.

WHICH FROG IS THE SMALLEST?

One of the smallest frogs in North America is the Little Grass Frog. It is about the size of one of your fingernails.

WHAT IS THE LIFE CYCLE OF A FROG?

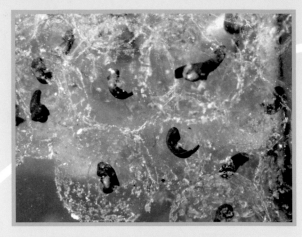

2. In each egg, a tiny tadpole begins to grow. After some time, the egg breaks open and the tadpole pops out.

1. Mother frog lays hundreds of eggs in the water.

3. Tadpoles have tails and look like little fish.

4. Soon legs grow. The tail gets smaller and smaller, until it is not there anymore.

5. Finally, a frog crawls onto land.

Wood Frog

21

LEARN MORE

BOOKS

Aronosky, Jim. *All About Frogs*. New York: Scholastic Press, 2002.

Miller, Sara Swan. *Frogs and Toads: The Leggy Leapers*. New York: Franklin Watts, 2002.

Taylor, Barbara. *Frogs and Snakes*. Columbus, Ohio: Peter Bedrick Books, 2002.

An American Bullfrog eats a ribbon snake.

WEB SITES

Enchanted Learning

<www.enchantedlearning.com>

Frog pictures to color, life cycle of the frog.

Frogland

<www.allaboutfrogs.org>

Weird frog facts, frogs in the news.

Kiddyhouse

<www.kiddyhouse.com/
 Themes/frogs/>

Frog feet, big and small frogs, frog stories.

Poison Dart Frog

INDEX

A Note About Reptiles and Amphibians:

Amphibians can live on land or in water. Frogs, toads, and salamanders are amphibians. Reptiles have skin covered with scales. Snakes, alligators, turtles, and lizards are reptiles.

Enslow Elementary, an imprint of Enslow Publishers, Inc.
Enslow Elementary® is a registered trademark of Enslow Publishers, Inc.

Copyright © 2008 by Carmen Bredeson

Library of Congress Cataloging-in-Publication Data

Bredeson, Carmen.
Fun facts about frogs! / Carmen Bredeson.
p. cm. — (I like reptiles and amphibians)
Includes bibliographical references and index.
ISBN 13: 978-0-7660-2788-6
ISBN 10: 0-7660-2788-0
1. Frogs—Juvenile literature. I. Title. II. Series.
QL668.E2B67 2006
597.8'9–dc22   2006006877

Printed in the United States of America

10 9 8 7 6 5 4 3 2 1

Photo Credits: © Gary Meszaros/Visuals Unlimited, pp. 7, 20B; © Ingrid VanDenBerg/Animals Animals; p. 12; © Joe McDonald/Visuals Unlimited, p. 9; © Ken Lucas/Visuals Unlimited, p. 21B; © Mark Moffett/Minden Pictures, p. 18; © Michael Redmer/Visuals Unlimited, pp. 11, 20T, 21T, 21M; © OSF/Hilary Pooley/Animals Animals, p. 8; © James Robinson/Animals Animals, p. 19; Shutterstock, p. 23; © Stephen Dalton/Minden Pictures, pp. 6, 16–17; © Warren Photographics, pp. 3, 4–5, 10, 15; © Zigmund Leszczynski/Animals Animals, pp. 1, 22, 24.

Cover Photograph: © David Aubrey / Science Photo Library

Series Science Consultant:
Raoul Bain
Herpetology Biodiversity Specialist
Center for Biodiversity and
Conservation
American Museum of Natural History
New York, NY

Series Literacy Consultant:
Allan A. De Fina, Ph.D.
Past President of the New Jersey
Reading Association
Professor, Department of Literacy Education
New Jersey City University
Jersey City, NJ